THIS BOOK BELONGS TO
The Library of

....

....

Did you like my book? I pondered it severely before releasing this book. Although the response has been overwhelming, it is always pleasing to see, read or hear a new comment. Thank you for reading this and I would love to hear your honest opinion about it. Furthermore, many people are searching for a unique book, and your feedback will help me gather the right books for my reading audience.

Thanks!

Table of Contents

Introduction

Recently, I became a proud member of the Keller Williams Luxury Community. It took a lot of hard work and constant grinding. But it's a REALTOR® designation I truly deserve.

Now, I'm getting calls from new agents asking me how I did it. Well, becoming a luxury real estate agent has its rewards. However, there are things you must keep in mind, or you may wind up spending more time backtracking than cashing checks.

I wrote this eBook to help new agents understand the pitfalls of getting into the real estate industry without being properly prepared. It's my personal journal that highlights the things people should do before stepping into the real property arena. These are thirty-three things I wish I had known as a new agent that would have gotten me a KW Luxury designation much sooner.

In this book, we'll discuss everything from choosing the right brokerage to marketing online and hiring the right staff to looking like luxury yourself. We'll also go over ways to build your new upscale realtor business.

From there, we dive into some exceptionally unique ways to market luxury real estate. Then, we wrap it all up with some effective tips for new agents marketing luxury homes. Learn how to build your new brand as an entrepreneur to tap into the upscale real estate market sooner than later.

I've been flipping houses for over twelve years now. In January 2018, I decided to take my house rehabbing business to the next level and became a licensed real estate agent in the State of Georgia. Today, I primarily work with Atlanta luxury home sellers under the Keller Williams brokerage. This is my story.

Launching Your Luxury Real Estate Career as a New Agent

As we all sit back and wait for the launch of upcoming Atlanta-based real estate reality TV shows like VH1's *Hollywood of the South* and OWN's *Ladies Who List*, I decided now is a good time to document some of the mistakes I made when I launched my new career as an agent. Some of these bloopers were direct reasons why it took me so long to conquer the luxury market.

Becoming an agent may seem exciting. Many new agents think of real estate sales as a solid career choice. So many people dream of becoming entrepreneurs and working for themselves—and real estate offers such opportunities. I remember popping champagne after cashing my first commission on the sale of a house. However, I also remember making some drastic mistakes that could have cost me *and my clients* some lucrative deals.

Unlike HGTV reality shows, which make selling real estate seem so simple, the hustle is real. From securing new sellers and buyers to following up on leads, there's so much work to be done in this game. And when it comes to the luxury market, consumers not only expect to be nurtured, but these high-end clients also want their agents to pamper and spoil them. Had I only known then what I know now.

In today's market, you must be willing to do more than just chase commissions. It's all about building your own personal and professional brands, both online and in-person… *locally*. You *must* create a name for yourself locally to succeed in this industry. Like my marketing strategist says:

You must put your face out there. The goal is for people to see you on the streets of Atlanta and think of you as a local celebrity!

---

33 Things Newbie Luxury Real Estate Agents Should Never Do

Thanks to my real estate mentors, I was prepped and trained thoroughly. So, I didn't make as many mistakes as typical newbies. However, there are many things I know now that I didn't know then that would have eliminated many errors and cut back on a lot of headaches. Plus, I would have been catapulted into the luxury real estate market long before now.

Here are thirty-one things I wish I knew as a new real estate agent trying to tackle Atlanta's luxury homes market:

1. Choosing the Wrong Brokerage

When I first started out, I chose to hang my license at my first brokerage for personal reasons. That wasn't necessarily a mistake. But after a while, I found that there were better options for me. Even though this broker is still my friend and mentor to this day, I had to do what was best for my future, my brand and my career.

Every brokerage is not the same. I wish I would've initially chosen a brokerage that provided more support after I first obtained my sales license. Don't get me wrong. I loved my original brokerage, but they weren't prepared to teach me what I needed to be successful in this business as a high-end real estate agent.

My original broker had classes for its agents. However, I was still working full-time and couldn't make the very few classes that it had to offer. Therefore, I never received the mentorship and guidance I needed to transition into a full-time agent who lists and sells luxury homes.

Moving Over to Keller Williams

That was… until I did my research and learned that Keller Williams (KW) is an industry leader. In fact, it is the largest real estate brokerage in North America. KW provides extensive training, both in-person and online, to help new and seasoned agents get to the finish line.

The brokerage also offers an entire suite of services for buyers and sellers, including, but not limited to:

Kelly Mortgage

KW offers a ZeroPlus loan program for anyone buying a KW listing or using a KW buyer's agent to purchase a home.

Keller Covered

KW provides a service that helps homeowners and buyers shop for and compare insurance quotes that best suit their needs.

Keller Offers

KW now provides all-cash offers to sellers who need to get out fast for various reasons, such as divorces or to avoid foreclosure. There are also programs for those needing repairs or upgrades to sell for higher prices or simply to remain in their homes.

Here are the three Keller Offers (KO) programs to choose from:

1. Cash Offer Program – Get preliminary cash offers for your home within 72 hours. Close escrow in under 90 days. No showings. No open houses. No coordinating repairs. No contingencies.
2. Ready to Stay Program – Choose from multiple finance options to get cash fast for home improvement projects. This makes it possible for you to remain in and enjoy your home without enormous upfront costs.

3. <u>Ready to Sell Program</u> – For those who are ready to sell, you can get cash and use it to fix up your home and get it ready for the market. Use the cash to improve your home's curb appeal, make needed repairs, upgrade appliances, declutter, etc…

As you can see, it's about much more than just training and support when it comes to choosing a brokerage firm. It's about giving clients options that make life easier for them, which helps KW agents sell homes faster.

Make sure the brokerage you select offers you and your clients what you need to succeed. Not everyone needs cash from KO to sell their homes. But having the option available provides luxury home buyers and investors improve their financial catalogs while freeing up other resources to do what needs to be done.

2. Not Having a Good Mentor

Good brokerages make it a point to provide each new agent with a mentor. If yours doesn't, I suggest searching for a real estate mentor outside of the brokerage. My first broker did a good job mentoring me, but I needed an outstanding mentor to get where I am today.

Just think about it. You may find yourself writing contracts at 10:00 PM on a Saturday night. Who do you call when you have questions? You need a mentor who will be there for you day and night… and definitely on the weekends because that's when sellers are available the most.

Here are some of the benefits of securing a good real estate mentor early on in your new career:

Accountability

Having someone to hold you accountable is key when you're building your new brand as an agent in the luxury housing market.

You need someone to help you set achievable goals and track your progress toward them.

Because you work independently in this business, procrastination is the enemy. A good real estate mentor should provide you with consistent reminders to take proactive, timely steps to advance your brand and business… because high-end clients know their value and *will* move on to the next agent.

Industry Knowhow

Your mentor gives you access to industry expertise and expert advice. An ideal mentor should have no less than five years of experience and provide you with one-on-one training.

Make sure your mentor has proven success in luxury real estate sales, as well as marketing. Check out the agent's reviews and make sure the professional has a record of closing luxury home transactions every year.

Professional Networking

As a professional agent, you must understand the value of networking with others within the industry, as well as vendors. Mentors teach you effective strategies for networking with others.

Your mentor should introduce you to some of their past clients to help you gain new leads. This person should also vouch for the work you do with new clients. In turn, you become even more influential in the industry while improving your reach within your local market. The goal is to become a local star whose face is recognizable within the luxury home community.

Support and Motivation

To be a great mentor, one must have a passion for and a willingness to teach others. These professionals must inspire and motivate new agents to take chances and step outside their comfort zones. This is the only way to succeed at engaging with sellers and buyers.

However, even with a great mentor in your corner, you *must* be prepared to put in the work. As a mentee, developing your unique brand and building your business is key to succeeding in the real estate market as an agent in the luxury arena.

3. Not Taking Contracts Courses

Contracts can be a nightmare for a new agent! I almost screwed a client over by having them sign the purchase agreement instead of just the counter document.

Unilateral Amendments can be nightmarish as well. I also neglected to send an eight-day unilateral agreement in time. Luckily for me, *and my client*, the alternate agent was nice enough to not take my client's earnest money. But this could've been a disaster.

Because of this, I recommend that every newbie find a contracts class and complete it immediately upon getting into the business. Ask your broker to refer you to one or check out the courses offered by the National Association of REALTORS® (NAR). The last thing you want to do is mess up a contract on a multi-million-dollar home.

4. Not Branding and Marketing Online

In today's real estate market, it takes much more than putting up "For Sale" and "Sold" signs, hanging door hangers and making cold calls to succeed. These days, advertising and marketing online are mandatory if you want to improve your reach and get qualified leads. Why? Because according to the NAR:

> *97% of all homebuyers used the internet in their home search.*

Personally, I've always hated social media. But many agents following these branding techniques are reaping large rewards from marketing themselves online. I wish I would've started my online branding campaign sooner.

Had I done so, I would have many more followers and my social media reach would be much farther than it is today. Also, had I spent more time publishing high-quality images and videos of my luxury listings, I would be more known in that market as a local agent.

Using Social Media for Branding

Social media is the best way to let the world know that you're a real estate agent. Just be careful not to use it as a way to publish sales content that doesn't provide value for potential clients.

Instead, you want to provide them with:

- Free seller and buyer tips
- Home design information
- Local market stats that answer questions and solve problems they have

This helps you develop long-lasting relationships while building trust with your target audience. So, when these high-end potential clients are ready to buy or sell, they'll always remember you, the local expert who always kept them informed.

Becoming a Social Media Star

Instagram, TikTok and Pinterest are quickly becoming the go-to social media sites when it comes to luxury real estate. Selling luxury homes requires building online brands while creating a following that brings you success. This requires awesome, high-resolution videos and images to immediately capture your audience's attention.

Relying on word of mouth client referrals alone just doesn't cut it in this business, especially for new agents with little to no closings under their belts. Social media helps you form valuable connections while marketing to "friends" online. Nurture – engage with – these leads properly, and many will become your clients someday.

Allow your social media platforms to show the real, yet professional, *you*. Your audience wants to see how you vibe and understand your professional expertise. This improves your chances of them choosing you as their trusted agent someday, versus choosing a random agent through Realtor or Zillow. These days, some of my most engaging posts feature me looking luxurious in my clients' extravagant homes.

NAR Stats on Social Media

According to a NAR study, social media is key to reeling in new clients and closing deals. Here are some of their key findings:

- 47% of real estate professionals credit social media for getting them the highest quality leads as opposed to other sources
- 77% of real estate pros actively utilize social media in one way or another for branding and engaging with their target markets
- 90% of Baby Boomers and 99% of Millennials start their searches for homes for sale online as opposed to personal referrals

Social Media Platforms for Realtors

So, what social media platforms are great for luxury real estate agents? Here are just a few:

- Facebook – Pages, groups and ads

- LinkedIn – Personal and business pages
- Instagram – Personal and business accounts, as well as IG stories
- YouTube – Video content, plus you can even get monetized for added income
- Pinterest – Personal and business accounts
- TikTok – Make personal connections with other professionals *and* potential clients
- Connected Investors – Allows real estate buyers, sellers and private investors to connect with each other online

5. Not Utilizing My Website for Branding

When I first launched KereenHenry.com, I just wanted to establish an online presence. I located my old marketer and had her write some webpage content and that was pretty much it. Every time I listed a home for sale, she would do some research on that local market and create a blog post or two for me to publish on my site.

Today, I realize how much of a mistake that was all these years later. There's no way anyone would ever see those posts to drive sales to the listings because search engines just don't work like that. The best way to get Google and its competitors to show your content in search results is to continuously publish fresh, new content.

Yes, you can create a decent online presence by being featured on your broker's website. And having listings on MLS will get your name on sites like Realtor.com and Zillow.com. But basically, you're essentially building their brands, not your own.

It's important to feature your listings on your own site and drive traffic to them by blogging regularly. You must also brand yourself SEO-wise as a *luxury* realtor by infusing related words into your content.

Real Estate SEO

What is SEO? It stands for search engine optimization. It's the process of attracting high-quality, relevant traffic to your website, blog or other online content via Google and other search engines. This relates to organic (unpaid) traffic, as opposed to paid advertising.

For real estate professionals, SEO is all about *local* traffic, versus marketing to the masses. You want to reach buyers and sellers who are either currently located in your local area or are interested in moving to or investing there. That means your target audience will be searching for properties using terms like "Atlanta luxury homes for sale" and other surrounding communities.

SEO keywords are extremely important for driving organic traffic to your content. These keywords should be infused in everything, including the following:

- Page titles
- Meta descriptions
- Subheadings
- Content
- Images
- URLs
- Link anchor text
- Social media
- Directories
- External listings
- Property descriptions

Building Your Own Brand

My advice to every new agent is to launch *your own* website and blog. Hire a professional to create informative and engaging content for your webpages that speaks directly to the high-end market.

Then, come up with a decent budget that allows that content marketer to provide you with at least five new blog posts each week, so you can publish Monday through Friday. Make sure this professional has SEO research skills. This helps them create content that your target market is currently searching for in Google and other search engines.

This will encourage search engines to send more valuable traffic to your site while improving your brand's online presence. Build an online reputation as *the* local go-to source for luxury real estate advice, tips, tricks and entertainment.

6. Thinking I'm Really a Salesperson

Guess what? Even though your official title is a real estate sales agent, you're not actually a salesperson. Why do I say that? Well, in this business, there is no hard selling. Although some agents do take part in this practice, they tend to quickly become irrelevant in this industry.

Effective luxury real estate sales are all about two things:

1. Finding the right buyer for a high-end seller's listing
2. Finding the perfect luxury home for a high-end buyer

That means it's your job to:

- Do initial inspections of homes
- Make recommendations for getting homes ready for the market
- Show homes to potential buyers and let them look around
- Allow buyers to make educated decisions they can live with for years to come
- Help sellers find the resources they need to move out of their homes at closing

No Hard Sells Needed

None of this involves hard sales. When an agent is too pushy, both buyers and sellers run away as quickly as possible. Buying a home is an extremely big purchase. Oftentimes, it's the biggest purchase most people ever make in life.

Give every client the chance to think about her/his likes and dislikes about a home and deeply consider the options. Never try to hard-sell clients or push them into purchases they may regret in the end. Your reputation depends on it. So do your online reviews!

7. Hiring the Wrong People

Hiring the right people to help you run your business and grow your brand is key. Not having a transaction coordinator at the beginning of my real estate career was harmful because it caused me to miss dates and contract deadlines. And extravagant clients really hate that.

Without good help, I was unorganized and that held me back from growing as a realtor. At some point, I hired a virtual assistant (VA). But she knew *nothing* about real estate, just like me. So, I spent a lot of time teaching her the business while trying to learn the processes myself.

Hire the Right Professionals

To this day, I love my VA. However, I feel like my business *was not* and still *is not* a priority for her. She's rarely willing to go the extra mile to ensure that she knows all things real estate. Even when there's something she can easily research herself on Google, I must "hold her hand" while spoon-feeding her the answers.

My advice to all newbies is to hire an assistant who actually knows the real estate industry, even if she has only been an agent's receptionist for a few years. Also, start building your brand immediately by hiring a professional marketer who's willing to take courses, participate in webinars, and do the research needed to understand the business better, as well as the specialized services you and your brokerage offer.

This person *must* know or have the desire to learn the local market. If not, you'll never reach, capture leads from or effectively nurture those potential high-end clients.

8. Not Using CRM Tools

From the very beginning, I should have been utilizing Customer Relationship Management (CRM) tools to collect contact information. Instead, I stored everything in my iPhone, which turned out to be a real problem when my marketer launched my email campaigns.

The contacts were imported into Mailchimp. Many were automatically flagged for various reasons. Then, when campaigns went out, so many users opted out and reported my emails as spam simply because they hadn't actually "opted-in" as email subscribers.

What is a CRM? It's a system that tracks more than just names, phone numbers, addresses and emails. They help you keep track of clients' birthdays, anniversaries, births, even deaths. This makes it easy to nurture these valuable leads with cards, gifts and awesome personalized emails.

I wish I would've spent more time collecting the information I needed from potential clients. Instead, here I am backtracking to get my marketer the info she needs to nurture my leads for me. So, use a CRM of some sort from day one. Today, I use the Keller Williams Command system for managing customer relationships with my high-end clients.

9. Not Nurturing My Leads

What is lead nurturing? In the real estate industry, it's the process of creating and strengthening relationships with sellers and buyers at each and every single phase of the sales funnel.

For your lead nurturing campaign to be successful, your communication and marketing efforts must address the following:

- Listening to your potential clients' needs
- Building trust with them by providing solutions to problems they are having
- Increase your brand awareness
- Maintain connections through regular engagement until they're ready to buy or sell

Lead nurturing campaigns are designed for communicating with each potential client and client on an individual level. Because of this, all of the content in each campaign should be personalized. The content *must* answer relevant questions your audience has to help them solve specific industry-related problems. This leads to long-term relationships.

Some campaign types include:

- Email campaigns
- Direct mail campaigns
- Online ad campaigns
- Social media posts

Although as a marketer, I've always known the importance of nurturing leads, until recently, I haven't done it consistently. One reason is that I simply didn't have the time. So, I've hired a marketer to take over many of the related tasks for me, especially my email campaigns, which are now being automated.

10. No Email Marketing

One of the most powerful marketing channels around is email marketing. It's a digital and direct marketing tactic that promotes your brand, your listings and your content via email campaigns.

Here are the top reasons why you should be utilizing email marketing campaigns:

Exceptional Communication Channel

According to experts, more than 99% of consumers check their emails every single day. No other communication channel can beat that stat.

List Ownership

Unlike the leads list many agents purchase from various companies, such as Corefact, your email list is 100% yours. It's unique and there is no other list like it. No one can take your leads away from you.

Outstanding Conversion Rates

Consumers who make purchases of products and services marketed via email spend 138% more than consumers who didn't receive email offers. As a matter of fact, the return on investment (ROI) for email campaigns is a whopping 4400%.

My Email Campaigns

Earlier this year, my marketer played around with a system called Drip. It was one of the cheapest on the market. However, the company doesn't offer landing pages or surveys. So, she recently switched back to Mailchimp.

According to her, these are some of the best benefits of using Mailchimp for email campaigns:

- Customer Journeys
- Transactional Emails
- Retargeting Ads
- Postcards
- Surveys
- Unique Integrations
    - Instagram Content Blocks
    - Google My Business
    - QuickBooks
    - SurveyMonkey
    - Eventbrite
    - Adobe Photoshop
    - Canva

Just keep in mind that your target audience is high-end homeowners and profit-making buyers. That means your templates and emails should reflect their affluent lifestyles.

11. Not Hiring an Accountant ASAP

Unlike W2 workers, real estate agents receive commission checks with no taxes deducted. That means it's up to us to pay the required taxes and file the required documents each year or face consequences from the IRS, our states and other federal entities.

But as an agent, you simply don't have the time to take tax courses to learn how to do your own tax returns correctly. Most of us don't even know where to start when it comes to setting aside the proper amounts to pay each year. And when you're listing and selling multi-million-dollar homes, this could be a really big problem.

So, what's the simplest answer to this problem? Hire a professional accountant before you cash that first commission check. Your accountant will advise you on how much you need to put aside from each check for taxes, and where to store those funds so you don't comingle them with your net income.

12. Not Saving Receipts

Paperwork is key if you ever get audited by the IRS. You should save every single receipt, even if it's not related to your real estate business.

There are some amazing apps out there that allow you to scan receipts and store them in a cloud. That way, they are there when you need them no matter what.

13. Comingling Funds

This is an issue I *just* cleaned up, thanks to my accountant's insistence. I've spent pretty much my entire real estate career using my personal accounts to run my business. This creates a horrid mess come tax time.

Deductibles are important when filing your taxes. But if you're using personal bank accounts and credit cards to run your entrepreneurship, it's almost impossible to see at-a-glance what is what.

In the end, you'll find yourself paying, even more, to get your taxes done because your accountant must comb through everything looking for business deductions. Also, speak with this professional about creative ways to create these deductions, such as buying gifts for clients.

Keep Personal and Business Funds Separate

My advice to you is to open a business checking account immediately, even if it's not incorporated. Also, start building your business credit, even if the business is in your government name.

Comingling funds is a path to disaster. So, do the right thing from the beginning. Thank me later!

14. Expecting the Buying Process to Be Easy

Every week, people tune in to real estate shows like Property Brothers, Zombie House and Flipping Vegas to check out the house flipping process. But beware. These shows romanticize the processes of buying, improving and selling homes, which is just not realistic.

HGTV has been very instrumental in inspiring people to become newly licensed agents. They come into the business thinking the entire buying process is not only fast but that it happens almost overnight. This is all one big delusion.

Buying a Home Takes Time

In reality, it can take months, even years, to find the perfect home for a finicky buyer. Giving up is not an option if you want to get that good review. You must practice due diligence, no matter how long it takes, especially when dealing with high-end real estate.

Also, keep in mind that the negotiation process can be stressful if you let it. These things take time to settle too. And as the agent, it's your job to put out fires during the transaction, so you can get your client to the closing table—but in the end, your buyer will love you for getting them the keys to their extravagant dream homes.

15. Not Having Buyer and Seller Presentations

You need to develop killer presentations for both sellers and buyers. And you *must* practice those presentations over and over again. This is vital to your success because, as we all know, practice makes perfect, even in this industry.

The ultra-rich can be a very demanding demographic. You must be prepared and pay close attention to detail to meet these consumers' demands. Confusion tends to increase that demand, which is why your goal should be to anticipate any questions the client may have before it's even asked. That means you must be:

- Brief
- Organized
- Timely
- Specific

When you present your buying, listing and selling plans to potential clients, it's imperative that you answer each and every one of their questions flawlessly. Sometimes, I stand in the mirror and practice my presentations to ensure that my presentational flow is perfect.

I suggest keeping the presentation conversational. The last thing you want to do is bore your potential clients. Instead, make them feel like they are part of the conversation and answer all their questions thoroughly and professionally and with a glowing smile.

16. Launching Without Upfront Cash

There are multiple expenses when it comes to becoming a new luxury real estate agent. From licensing fees and training costs to MLS dues and promotional material, these expenses are vital to running a successful high-end real estate business. This industry is no "get rich quick" scheme. You get out of it what you put into it.

You can't count on your commission to cover everything you need upfront, because, without the right tools, you probably won't make the sale to get the commission in the first place. That's why experts, including myself, suggest having no less than six months' worth of savings in the bank before launching your new career. No one can predict when you'll reap the benefits of your first high-end sale.

Expenses to Expect Early On

These are just some of the expenses you should prepare to cover as a newbie in this field:

- Real estate dues
- Insurance
- Cell phone
- Brokerage fees
- Auto expenses
- Brand Marketing
- Listing marketing

17. Not Being Prepared to Hustle

For agents, the real estate game is all about the hustle. Yes, you can use social media to get exposure for your brand and your listings. However, there's much more to being successful than posting pics of listings and utilizing cool hashtags.

At some point, you will need to find your own professional niche in the luxury industry. This may be:

- Divorce listings
- For sale by owners (FSBO)
- Inherited properties
- Vacant properties
- Expired luxury listings

…or whatever you find works best for you. If you want to get the job done, you must be prepared to:

- Knock on doors
- Make cold calls
- Send out emails

- Mail out postcards
- Conduct showings
- Host open houses

And don't forget the power of following up. You need to do this with each prospective client at least 5-10 times before securing the listing or making the sale.

18. Not Making Phone Calls

Never fear calling them on the phone, even if it sounds like you're bugging them. It's all worth it in the end if you want to make that commission down the line. You need to network and meet as many new people as you possibly can to succeed in real estate.

For many, especially Millennials, using digital technology is much easier than making phone calls. But many potential clients prefer calls over text messages, emails and social media messages, especially Baby Boomers.

Utilize the Phone No Matter What

Since I became a real estate agent, I've made so many phone calls that *I'm* even shocked about it. Now, I have no problem picking up my cell or office phone and dialing away to reach out to potential clients who may have selling or buying on their minds.

Step outside your comfort zone and push yourself to make introductions to strangers via calls and in-person. Use your confidence in yourself to secure new potential high-end clients everywhere you go, from the grocery store to the coffee house to the gym.

17. Not Being Ready for the Administrative Work

There are many moving parts when trying to build your brand and run a successful real estate business. You'll need to do much more than just showing houses and placing your listings in MLS to reach those high-end consumers.

Some days you'll find yourself making follow-up calls and answering tons of emails. Other days you will be devoted to taking courses, doing market research and personalizing marketing plans.

All of this requires administrative work that you may or may not have time for in the end. So, keep track of the menial tasks that you can outsource to others over time. This frees you up to spend more time looking for new leads and nurturing the ones you already have.

Learn and Teach

I suggest learning every single one of these admin tasks until you have them down pat. Then, hire an assistant who knows the business and is willing to learn the admin tasks you already know how to perform to perfection.

This is important because anything can happen. So, if there's an emergency, you can temporarily take over the tasks yourself while training a new assistant to get the job done for you. Always remember, you can't teach what you don't know.

18. Not Utilizing Downtime

This time three months ago, I had one buyer with a mansion in escrow, and three active seller listings. Today, those that haven't closed escrow are under contract. This leaves me with quite a bit of downtime right now.

So, what do I do while my marketer works on helping me secure new listings? I'm taking time out to up my game by taking Keller Williams Cash Offer courses, as well as quite a few others.

In fact, I've made it my goal to take at least two courses each week. This will help me stay up to date on the current market, new products and services and real estate marketing trends.

Always Leverage Downtime

Education is key. But there's much more you can do to leverage your downtime. Here are seven good examples of things to do to help build your brand as a luxury agent:

1. Integrate your CRM with your website and transaction management system
2. Work on your lead funnel by customizing client emails, scripts, and videos
3. Launch your nurturing campaign to keep the lines of communication open with potential clients
4. Go hard with your social media campaigns, strategies, and advertising
5. Give back as an ambassador of your local community by volunteering, as I did with the NSN Atlanta Hope for Domestic Violence campaign
6. Create lead magnets to capture emails from potential clients in exchange for free webinars and eBooks to help sellers with their listings
7. Improve your email campaigns so they meet the needs of more than one dynamic

19. Not Building Long-Lasting Relationships

In the beginning, new agents will jump at just about any opportunity to secure a buyer or a listing. But it's important that your clients work well with your personality. Let your personality shine while being your true, authentic self.

Keep in mind that in many cases, the first impression clients get of you will probably come from your online presence. Locally, your social presence matters and people want to feel a connection with you on these platforms, even in the high-end market.

So, if you're an agent with a bunch of tattoos, don't hide them. Instead, target buyers and sellers that either love tattoos as well or could care less about them one way or another. And how do you do that? By not hiding them in the first place.

Building Personal-Professional Connections

Your goal is to build professional, yet personal, relationships with your potential and active clients. You want to ensure that you're their trusted go-to source for all things luxury real estate. And keep in mind that your job doesn't necessarily end at closing.

Some clients may still need your assistance after getting their keys for various reasons, like finding:

- Plumbers
- Interior designers
- Landscapers
- Gardeners
- Roofers
- Painters
- Electricians

Providing Free Resources

I provide each of my sellers with a pre-selling guide to help them prep their homes for the market. And I also provide each buyer with a post-buying guide, so they don't have to struggle while looking for good, quality help within their new local communities.

These guides include names, websites, emails and phone numbers of vendors and other professionals in their areas that have proven themselves to provide quality work. This alone makes me a one-stop shop for both sellers and buyers while setting me apart from my competing local agents.

Blogging is also key to success here. Publishing blog posts that entertain, educate and inform your target market helps improve your online reach while targeting luxury homeowners and buyers looking for those homes.

A professional marketer will do the SEO research needed to determine what your target clients are searching for online to solve specific problems they're currently having. Use your blog to create online content that answers questions that solve those specific problems.

20. Expecting Not to Work Long Hours

Many new agents dream of the days when they can quit their 9-to-5 jobs and put in fewer hours selling real estate. However, this is a myth. And I wish I had known that early on in the game.

Yes, the real estate game gives you the chance to be your own boss. However, if you think you'll be working when you want to right out of the gate, you're sadly mistaken. Spending long days at Piedmont Park listening to bands play while kids run around having fun is not in your near future as a newbie. If you want to win those high-end contracts, you must put in the work.

Prepare to Become a Night Owl

You'll find that since most of your clients work full-time jobs or run businesses themselves, most of your interactions with them will be after normal business hours. Most sellers and buyers can't show and view properties until well after 5:00 PM during the week or on weekends only.

And when you don't have properties to view and show, there are many other things you need to do to improve your business and your brand's reach, such as:

- Take courses
- Attend webinars
- Write content
- Attend local events
- Visit other agents' open houses

Just be prepared to put in full-time hours if you want to gather up those full-time commission checks because high-end clients expect high-end customer service.

21. Expecting to Sell and Get Paid Overnight

At times, you may be lucky enough to bump into a client that's ready to sell now. You just happened to call, email or send them a postcard at precisely the right time. But typically, it won't be that easy.

Building a trustworthy relationship with a client can take months, sometimes even years. Oftentimes, the homeowner just isn't ready to sell yet. But with the right nurturing, when the homeowner *is* ready to sell, you'll be the agent they want to work with to get their home sold.

The Work Continues

Then, once you secure the listing, there's even more work to do. You may need to help your client:

- Find a new home
- Locate a qualified buyer to purchase the listing
- Deal with contracts and negotiations on both ends
- Wait for both escrows to close

All of this takes time, even when you're working with all-cash buyers. Closings are not fast processes. They often take months. So, in order to secure the client's positive reviews and referrals, you must continue nurturing the relationship until well after escrow closes and your commission checks are cashed to ensure continued success in this business.

In the beginning, I made the mistake of thinking once escrow closes, our relationship is over. But with continued nurturing, such as birthday and holiday emails, cards and gifts, I've found that some past clients remember me during that divorce sale or when their loved ones ask if they know a good agent. Just make sure that your nurturing is as high-end as the listings.

22. Thinking the Entire Commission Is Mine

I've always known that every broker gets a cut of each of its agents' commissions. Yet, many new agents come into the game not realizing this. Yes, there's good money to be made in this industry. But until you decide to become a broker yourself, you'll always have to share a piece of the pie.

However, once you find the right broker for your real estate brand, you'll start to build a virtually unlimited income for yourself. With the right training, tools and frame of mind, you could even become a millionaire selling multi-million-dollar real estate someday.

Just be sure to remain a support system for your potential and past clients, as well as friends, family and local community members. When the day comes that they're ready to buy or sell, they'll turn to you for advice. Patience is key in the luxury property business.

23. Not Being Prepared for Courtroom Visits

Although this has never happened to me... knock on wood... I've watched multiple agents and brokers get subpoenaed to court for various real estate-related reasons. In one situation, a colleague of mine was acting as a listing agent for a woman in the midst of a heated divorce.

She and her soon-to-be ex-husband couldn't agree on their home's value or how much they should list it for on the market. So, there my colleague was being called into court to tell the judge the property's true value.

Then, there was another colleague whose seller gave her incorrect information that was relayed in the listing's description. This ultimately led to the agent being subpoenaed to court to answer to the buyer's attorney.

The judge advised her to never again write up a listing without double-checking the information that the seller provided. We all live and learn!

24. Not Understanding That Buyers Can Be Liars

In sales, there's an old saying, "buyers are liars." Of course, this is not true for every buyer. But it's true in many cases. The phrase refers to the fact that buyers tend to say they want one thing, then they go out and buy something completely different.

During the beginning of my career, there were many times when I showed a buyer the exact house she/he claimed to want, yet didn't buy it for one reason or another. Then, later, I ended up speaking with the person during a follow-up just to hear her/him say, "I really should have purchased that home."

Understanding Buyers' Fears

In most cases, buyers don't buy "that perfect home" simply because they are afraid. Buying a home is one of the biggest purchases most consumers make in life, especially when you're talking luxury real estate. So, fear is completely understandable, although wasting your time as an agent is not.

Just be patient and keep following up with the "perfect" listings for them to view. Eventually, they'll conquer their fears and go ahead and take the leap. And you'll be right there to guide them through the entire buying process from beginning to end.

25. Spending Before the Commission Check Clears

Getting a fat commission check is no excuse for going on a spending spree or racking up new, unaffordable bills, trying to live a better life before it's time. Commissions are one-time payments. That means you should use them to ensure that your bills are paid for the long haul just in case you don't secure another one any time soon.

Most Americans live check-to-check. This includes high-end real estate agents. You never know when the next one is coming for sure. Why? Because even though a property may be "under contract," the deal can still fall apart at any phase of the transaction.

Until closing day comes and both the seller(s) and buyer(s) have signed on the dotted line, the deal is *not* final. So, wait until the check clears your business bank account before spending against it. And by all means, don't spend it all at one time… *just in case*.

26. Not Carrying Myself with Confidence

When I first became an agent, I was scared to:

- Make phone calls
- Visit clients' homes
- Write contracts
- Negotiate with other agents
- Actively promote *me* as a realtor on social media

But people continued working with me because they were unaware of my fears. I walked with confidence and held my head high at all times, like the luxurious agent I was aspiring to be.

In this case, I did something right. And I advise you to do the same. People are attracted to professionals who carry themselves with good posture and lots of confidence. Show clients, agents and vendors that you respect yourself and have confidence in your ability to compete in the high-end homes market. You must look, feel and carry yourself like luxury to compete for luxury listings and high-end buyers.

27. Not Putting on My Best Game Face

Even though I've always carried myself with good posture and confidence, sometimes I slipped up a bit in the beginning when it came to my game face. But my original broker mentored me well, showing me the ropes while helping me learn how to hide the look of fear.

In this business, making sales means setting yourself apart from your competitors, which are other local agents. There is so much competition in the luxury real estate business that you *must* find ways to do things differently and better than your colleagues if you want to land those valuable listings.

Never Let Them See You Sweat

Don't focus on the competition itself. This may lead you to burn important bridges with others in the industry who could be great assets to you later in your career. Since you're all working in the same local market, there's no telling when or how many times you may have to work with those same people again in the future.

And never let "them" see you sweat… *ANY* of them… not your prospects, clients, competitors, vendors or the people who work for you. Find the support network you need to help you keep going. And always wear your best game face because high-end clients can sense fear and prefer working with agents that walk with confidence.

28. Not Telling the World 'I'm a Realtor Now'

Don't be scared to tell everyone you know and meet that you're an upscale real estate agent. Remember how excited you were when you received your license? Carry that excitement around with you each and every day.

Just keep in mind that, unlike religion and politics, people actually enjoy chatting about real estate and the market as a whole. So, be the expert in their lives prepared to answer their questions about the current local and national markets and luxury property trends.

Rejoice About Your New Career

As a new agent, you want to scream about your new career from the highest mountaintop. Do just that! And know that in the real world, that mountaintop equates to social media and other online platforms.

So, go ahead and launch your new realtor website and start blogging about high-end real estate. Start your new social media business pages, groups and profile. And start bragging away!

29. Not Realizing Lenders Make the Real Estate World Go Round

Lenders mean everything in this industry. Without lenders, there is no financing. And without financing, most buyers can't afford to purchase a home. Why? Well, let's face it. How many people have $400K sitting in the bank available to spend on one piece of property?

Oftentimes, buyers look to their buyers' agents to refer them to good lenders. Make sure you have more than one within your network because different buyers have different needs and not every lender offers every program or package. And remember, not every lender deals with upscale properties.

Lender Nightmares

Working with a buyer who has a bad lender is not only a nightmare for the buyer and the seller, but it's a nightmare for you as the agent as well. From outrageous closing costs to extensive closing delays, bad lenders will have you pulling your hair out by the time the home closes escrow.

However, referring your client to a fantastic lender with a reputation for easy, fast and fair closings solves problems before they ever arise. So, be sure to continuously form healthy, professional relationships with awesome lenders in the high-end market just to make your own life easier.

30. Not Researching My Local Market

Remember when the bubble burst back in 2006 and 2007? Everyone was interested in learning about national and local real estate markets, from investors and agents to homeowners and marketers. Luckily for me, I wasn't in the game yet. But this helped me understand the value of research.

However, when I started my new career as an agent, this newfound knowledge went right out the door. Between learning the ropes and going through training, I never even thought about researching my local market. Truth be told, I hadn't even decided where that was just yet, short of it being in the Atlanta Metropolitan area.

Choosing a Market

Now that I'm a much more seasoned agent, I understand the value of choosing a specific market to work in and learning everything I can about it. When a potential buyer calls me about a listing in my market, it's important that I already know as much about it as possible.

Yes, I can always follow up with calls and emails. But having at least a little information in front of me about the area and its market makes me the "with it" realtor who knows about upscale listings in her local area.

Know Your Market

So, be sure to research daily or at least weekly. Go through MLS, Zillow, Realtor and other platforms to find out what's available in the multi-million-dollar home arena. Check out local high-end FSBOs. And investigate upscale vacant properties you see while driving through town.

Learning about local luxury listings before a potential buyer calls not only gives you a leg up, but it keeps you informed on comparables and other details you may need later. This sets you apart from other agents in your market.

31. Not Realizing How Fun Real Estate Is

I must admit, real estate sales can be a stressful career. However, I've never enjoyed any other career more than I do this one. In the beginning, I was a bit anxious, especially when I quit my job to do this full-time. But once I got into the groove, there was no turning back for me.

These days, I spend my time:

- Showing properties
- Dealing with inspection issues
- Staging homes
- Writing and negotiating contracts

- Capturing and nurturing leads
- Marketing listings
- Engaging with my audience on social media

And guess what? I enjoy every single minute of it!

Making My Mark

Each and every day, I wake up thankful for another day to get in the game and make my mark in this industry. I now know my calling. And because of that, I have a passion for what I do as a Keller Williams Luxury Community member.

So, learn as much as you can as a newbie now. But remember, upscale real estate is fun when you have the right tools and people in your corner to help you succeed.

12 Ways to Build Your New Upscale Realtor Business

You're finally here. And it's a bittersweet moment that triggers feelings of both excitement and stress dancing around in your gut. One part of you is thrilled about starting your new journey in life. The other part is confused about exactly where to start.

If you're thinking about becoming a self-made millionaire as a real estate agent, now is the prime time. Unlike planting a tree, growing your entrepreneurial status in this industry takes hard work, but it doesn't take decades to mature.

The high-end property market has its ups and downs. One month the news reports show we're in a buyer's market with record-low mortgage finance rates. And the following month we hear that it's a seller's market with a shortage of homes for buyers to choose from overall.

Don't let conflicting statistics confuse you or keep you from doing what it takes to succeed in this industry. Use these branding tips to help you discover who you are as a new realtor.

Here are a few more tips to help you start your endeavor as a new realtor in the upscale real estate game:

1. Create a Business Plan

Although, as a real estate agent, you work under a brokerage, you are still an independent contractor (in most cases). That means that *you* are your brand. That makes *you* not only an entrepreneur but an actual business as a whole.

Therefore, it's important that *you* - your brand… your business - have a business plan to keep you on track. This tool is considered a business's "roadmap to success," something you *must* have to provide good, quality service to upscale clients.

Its purpose is to help you convey an effective strategy for starting your business. The goal is to define your most important luxury business goals, then determine how you'll achieve them, step-by-step.

Benefits of Having a New Agent Business Plan

Basically, as a newbie, you can look at your business plan as an at-a-glance guide to keep you on track when it comes to achieving your goals in the high-end market. This is what a good plan for a new realtor should convey:

- Where you/your brand/your business are today
- Where you/your brand/your business want to be
- How you/your brand/your business plan to get there
- How to measure performance (milestones, sales per quarter, etc…)
- When to check and evaluate where you/your brand/your business are
- At what point you must make changes and corrections for better results

A Business Plan Creates Clarity and Transparency

When making important decisions about building your brand and your business in general, having clarity about key aspects of its operations is important. These attributes may be anything from investments to raising capital to marketing to leasing in upscale communities.

Once your business starts growing, you won't have time to do and remember everything. A good business plan will help you keep track of your most critical goals, milestones and priorities. That way, you know what to focus on at all times as you reel in those luxury real estate clients.

A Business Plans Helps with Target Marketing

Your marketing should never be "all over the place." The business's marketing goals should be clearly defined. So should your:

- Target market
- Target audience
- Target clients

Write out a clear strategy that details your planned promotion techniques to ensure your content and ads get out in front of the right people in the right market. A good business plan provides key information about the marketing strategy. It should do so clearly enough that even an admin can take over the job when needed.

A Business Plan Assists with Funding Support

What happens when you start making some money in this business and decide you want to start buying investment properties? Will you have all the capital you need to purchase that multi-family unit all alone? Will you want to take on the entire risk of investing in that fixer-upper without a partner?

If the answer to either one is, "no," then, this tip is for you. A good business plan helps answer very important questions like these. They are questions that capital investors, banks and other lenders ask before extending credit or becoming investors.

These questions are related to things like revenue generation, profitability gross proceeds, etc… So, keep your accountant informed and your plan up to date just in case you need funding for that lucrative luxury property project you want to take part in.

A Business Plan Helps You with Hiring Staff

When the time comes for you to hire a full-time assistant, marketer, ghostwriter, etc… Don't make the mistake I did and not vet the talent properly. Bringing in the right key players at precisely the right time ensures that your business grows in a healthy manner while freeing up your time to do what you do best as an agent.

Once again, you can't do everything. By the time you become a seasoned, successful agent, you should already have a high-quality team in place working in the background while you shine at the forefront. So, what does this have to do with a business plan?

Another purpose of a business plan is to help your staff understand your business better. It lays out the vision of the company – *you* – and how you plan to achieve your business goals. You should also explain how employees can use their own roles to contribute to this to improve your chances of landing those upscale listings.

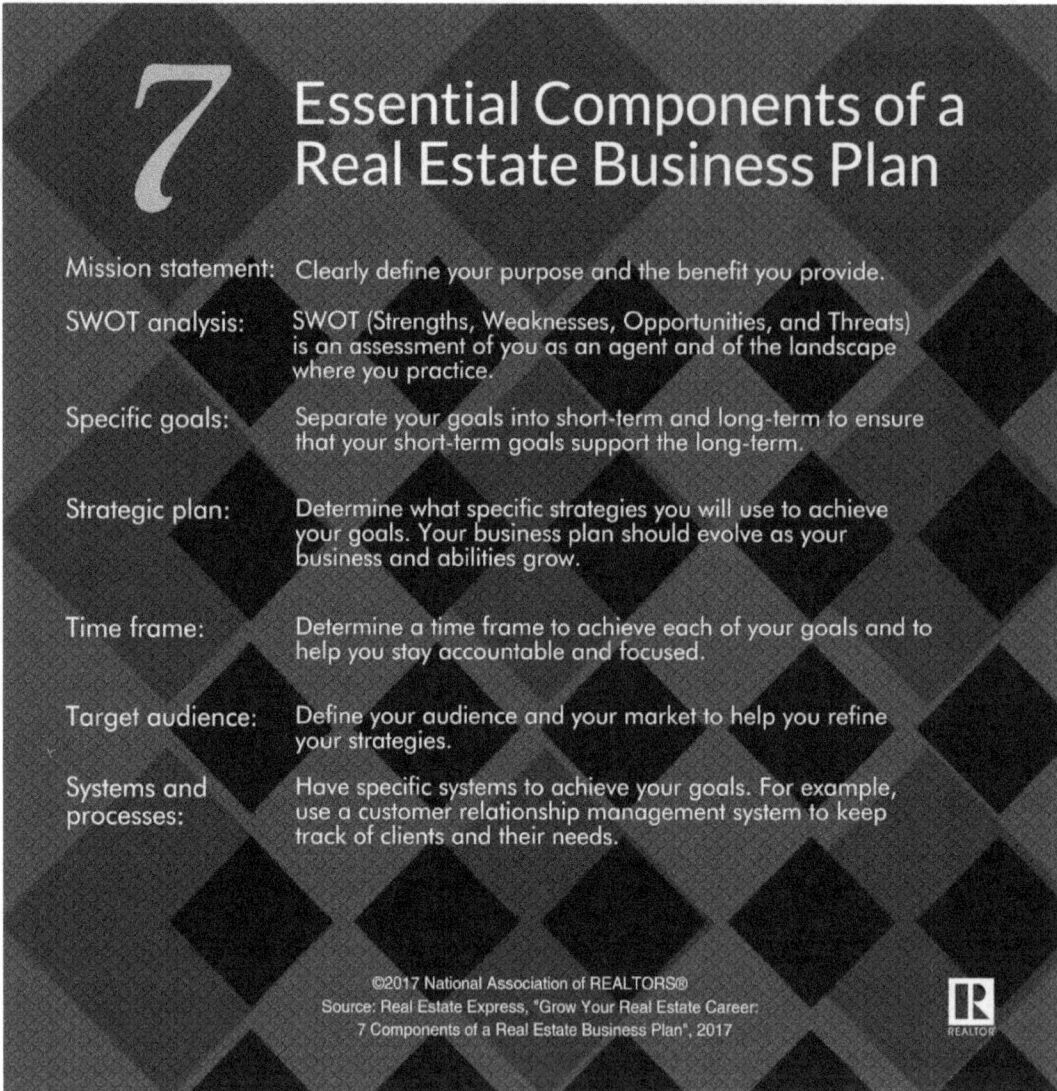

7 Essential Components of a Real Estate Business Plan

Mission statement: Clearly define your purpose and the benefit you provide.

SWOT analysis: SWOT (Strengths, Weaknesses, Opportunities, and Threats) is an assessment of you as an agent and of the landscape where you practice.

Specific goals: Separate your goals into short-term and long-term to ensure that your short-term goals support the long-term.

Strategic plan: Determine what specific strategies you will use to achieve your goals. Your business plan should evolve as your business and abilities grow.

Time frame: Determine a time frame to achieve each of your goals and to help you stay accountable and focused.

Target audience: Define your audience and your market to help you refine your strategies.

Systems and processes: Have specific systems to achieve your goals. For example, use a customer relationship management system to keep track of clients and their needs.

©2017 National Association of REALTORS®
Source: Real Estate Express, "Grow Your Real Estate Career:
7 Components of a Real Estate Business Plan", 2017

Image By National Association of REALTORS®

For assistance writing a professional business plan for your new luxury real estate brand, check out these free resources from the US Small Business Administration.

2. K.I.S.S. and Automate, Automate, Automate

Passive income allows you to make money while you're asleep. In that same regard, automation helps your business run smoothly, even when there's no one actively working on it.

Think about those friendly chats you have had online with your web host or bank. In the beginning, your questions are answered almost immediately. Then, after a while, the answers slow down.

That's because you were originally chatting with a bot. Those AI chatbots are designed to use keywords to *automatically* help answer your questions. If they can't, then and only then, will you be connected to a human representative.

These days, real estate agents use the same type of technology to handle property management requests and answer simple questions from leads. There is a boatload of things you can do to automate your marketing, operations, payroll and more.

Subscribe to my blog for an upcoming series on real estate agent automation tools.

3. Market Yourself as a Brand and a Business

Remember that *you* are your brand and your business is *you*. Now, it's time to start figuring out what that means for you professionally. Ask yourself these questions to help you understand your brand better:

- Who are you as an agent?
- Who do you want to be as an agent?
- What do you want your brand to be known for?
- Who would benefit most from that (target market)?
- Where are these people located? (state, county, city, community)
- How can you reach them (offline, online, which platforms)?

- Why should they choose you over your competitors?

Please know that these answers may change over time as you grow into your new business. So, write down your answers and tweak them whenever necessary to track your growth and progress.

Steps to Branding Your New Brand

In the meantime, it's time to start branding you as a real estate agent who means business and has a true passion for luxury homes. Here are the basic steps to getting started:

- Create a logo
- Purchase a domain name
- Create an email account using your *own* domain name (not Gmail or your broker's)
- Launch your responsive website and blog
- Get personalized business cards with your logo, website and own domain email

4. Personalize a Lead Generation Plan

A lot of people get into this game thinking they'll succeed simply because they say, "*I'm a people person.*" However, many of the top agents in the country are the complete opposite of that. Having a love for people can help your career. But you'd be shocked to learn just how many of the best agents in the US are shy loners.

So, how do they work with buyers and sellers when you're an introvert? Simple. Just be yourself.

Not all consumers look for friendliness when choosing an agent. Most want and need their reps to have empathy, skills and be authentic. That means, if you're an introvert, don't worry about it. Just be yourself and you'll still pull in high-end clients who care as little about small talk and chit-chat as you do.

Instead of concentrating on your weaknesses, put your energy into improving the strengths you already possess. In the real estate business, that equates to creating a lead generation strategy that effectively works for your type of personality, no matter what it is.

In other words, if you're an extrovert, then you should be focusing on knocking on doors in upscale communities and making cold calls to high-end consumers. However, if you have a more analytical personality, you may get better results from pay-per-click (PPC) ads and social media posts instead.

5. Take Local Branding & Marketing Seriously

As a realtor, building your brand is all about becoming known within your *local* community. That's where you want to carve out a place for your brand to shine because that's where your sellers live and your buyers plan to move.

Don't be fooled by SEO fanatics in India calling and emailing with promises of getting your brand on the first page of Google. They have no idea how to market an entrepreneur *locally*. For one reason, they don't know your *local* market. So, they have no idea what your target market is searching for online.

Secondly, they don't grasp that your competition is *right in your backyard*. So, ranking for keywords like "best real estate agent" won't help you in the long run. Instead, you need to rank for keywords like, "best luxury seller agent <your city>" and other more narrowed down phrases.

The same thing goes for social media branding and marketing where keywords work in conjunction with hashtags to help you reach the right audience. You must use keywords, phrases and hashtags that potential buyers and sellers in *your local area* are using on social media platforms to find awesome upscale realtors like you!

6. Tell Your Story

Knowing your story and telling it online is essential if you want to succeed in this business. But deciding *how* to convey your story to your target audience is not always as simple as it sounds. To determine what you should share about yourself as an agent, ask yourself some vital questions, like:

- Why did you decide to get into the real estate industry? For example:
    - Because it's quick to enter into with just a couple of courses and one big test?
    - Because you enjoy helping people get into the homes of their dreams?
    - Because you like staging homes and negotiating contracts?
- What sets you apart from other agents in your local community?
- Why should buyers and/or sellers choose you over your competitors?
- What drives you to work hard at what you do every single day?
- Specifically, what are you trying to accomplish as a local agent?

Sit down and come up with answers to all these questions. And be sure that your story behind *why* you became an agent is convincing and powerful. You may need to dig deep and do some serious soul searching. But it's vital to your career that you define:

- Who you are
- Who you want to help
- What you have to offer them
- Where they are located

- How you can help them
- Why you're trying to help them
- Why you're the best agent for the job

Knowing the answers to these questions will improve your confidence now instead of later. And that's a very big deal for a new agent trying to land high-end clients in the luxury real estate market.

7. Build Your Personal Brand on Social Media

For years, I've watched seasoned brokers see declines in listings and sales simply because they ignore the power of social media. But believe it or not, that's where your qualified leads can be found and reached with very little effort.

Ryan Matthew Serhant is a real estate broker who also stars on Bravo's reality TV shows *Million Dollar Listing New York* and *Sell It Like Serhant*. This professional realtor said it best when asked about social media marketing for agents:

"It's the biggest gift salespeople have ever been given."

Seasoned Broker Mistakes

Many brokers who have been in this business for decades just don't see the true value of social media for realtors. Therefore, they don't push their new agents to create and build their personal brands on platforms like Facebook and Instagram.

However, this is one of the most powerful ways to build trust with your target audience. Branding yourself on social media is much more effective for reaching potential sellers and buyers that actually need your help than bombarding your family and friends with cold calls and hard-sell messages they don't like, want or need.

Building your social media audience takes a bit more than just posting regularly. You need to find creative ways to engage with your target audience to:

- Capture more leads
- Nurture your leads
- Convert your leads into actual clients

Luckily for me, Keller Williams is all about innovation. I've been trained to use social media to captivate my followers while building relationships with them. It's one of the simplest ways to build an audience and connect and engage with them.

Learning What to Post

Personally, I've found that my most engaging posts are videos that have nothing to do with my listings. My audience enjoys watching clips of me doing simple things, like coming home from a hard days' work, taking off my pricey, Christian Louboutin Red Bottoms heels, popping open an expensive bottle of champagne and hanging out on my balcony enjoying the view.

Why? Simply because these videos show them the *personal…human…* side of me, versus the hard-selling real estate agent. I convey the idea of "upscale" in these videos, which immediately captures the attention of my target market.

And what about my real estate posts? Truth be told, they prefer my announcements about "JUST SOLD" properties more than my hard selling "JUST LISTED" posts.

Why? Once again, those "JUST SOLD" posts tend to be more on the personal side. Therefore, they enjoy them more because they've built virtual relationships and "friendships" with me and truly want to see me succeed.

Build Virtual Relationships

It's all about building online relationships with your audience and making them feel like they know you. No, you may not capture qualified leads or find new high-end listings early on in the brand-building process.

However, when the locals you engage with online are ready to buy or sell, they'll remember the agent with those adorable puppies or those engaging videos showing off her own home on social media.

Use a mixture of posts to capture leads online. Create posts that immediately capture your audience's attention as well as personal posts they can relate to themselves. This helps you come across as a professional who is also trustworthy, genuine and relatable, traits upscale clients value most.

8. Launch an Awesome Website

Piggybacking off of your broker's website will *not* set you apart from others at your brokerage or your local competitors. To brand yourself as a great luxury agent, you must have your own website, which gives you full control over the content you publish and the message you convey to your target audience.

Benefits of Having Your Own Site

Owning your own upscale real estate platform gives you the power to:

- Define your own personal and professional brands
- Generate qualified leads using your own lead capturing methods
- Nurture your leads *your way* while increasing conversion rates

- Convert your leads using email marketing and other creative tools

Let's say you decide to simply use the agent page created on your broker's website as your branding tool instead of launching your own website. Then, one day you decide to change brokerages.

Now what? You've essentially left all your online branding behind and must start from scratch again.

When I changed brokerages, it didn't impact my online brand. Why? Because KereenHenry.com was mine to keep forever. All I had to do was make a few changes to my Home and About pages to reflect the Keller Williams brand. That's why it's so important that you build a home base for your brand that you have full control over and can continue building throughout the life of your career.

Contact me if you have any questions about building a website for your real estate brand and business.

9. Team Up with Other Real Estate Agents

Oftentimes, new agents fear teaming up with other local agents simply because they don't want to split their commissions. But this is a vital mistake. Creating your own network of agents to team up with will ultimately help you grow your business while increasing your overall income. This is especially true in the high-end property arena.

Here are some of the benefits of utilizing the services of other agents to build your local reputation and sell more homes:

- Helps you get a better idea of what's happening in your local market within your entire region instead of the tiny area you're currently working in
- Gives you access to people who may have gone through or specialize in situations you have yet to deal with as a

new agent

- Helps you gain insight into how to deal with specific issues that may arise at some point in your career
- Gives you an advantage by helping you learn from the experience, knowledge and clientele of other more seasoned agents
- Allows you to pool resources, learn new skills and work with more than one client at the same time

Yes, oftentimes, this method does require sharing your commission with other agents. But just imagine how many more clients you gain access to by working with other agents along the way.

10. Solve Rich People Problems

Affluent consumers are always getting bombarded with sophisticated marketing campaigns. They are a busy group that simply doesn't have time for unnecessary "digital noise" in their lives. Therefore, when marketing to the elite, your content must be amazing and it must immediately show them how you and your brand fit into their lives.

They make decisions to work with specific brands fairly quickly. So, your message must clearly demonstrate exactly what problem you can solve for them. This helps you stand out from your competition within the luxury home industry.

Types of Problems the Elite Have

Wondering what type of problem you can solve for a rich consumer looking to sell or buy real estate? Well, here's a quick list of common issues the upper-class deal with to help you get your juices flowing:

- Asset appraisal
- Asset preservation
- Asset privacy

- Asset protection
- Banking
- Development
- Land use
- Legacy planning
- Legally avoiding taxes
- Lending
- Insurance
- Prenuptial agreements
- Real estate investing
- Real estate taxes
- Zoning

Choose one of these topics to make your main focus for helping with rich people's problems. Learn everything you can about the subject. Use the information to create informative blog posts to help drive traffic to your site.

You'll also find the information useful when you have a prospective luxury client that's having issues in that department. Just imagine how impressed the consumer will be to find out *you* are an expert in that arena.

In time, you'll be able to add this to your industry niche. Instead of just being a "luxury real estate agent," you can market yourself something like this:

"I help rich people increase their real estate portfolios while helping them keep their properties safe from lawsuits via asset protection services."

11. Market Wealthy Lifestyles… Not Listings

When marketing your listings, you must keep this in mind: Being wealthy is an actual lifestyle.

The best way to attract affluent buyers to your listings is to *visually show* them how their life would look if they lived in that particular home and community. You want to show them the luxurious lifestyle others in that surrounding area currently enjoy.

Things the Well-To-Do Like to Do

Some of the amenities rich people enjoy outside of their homes include:

- Beaches
- Lakes
- Golf courses
- Country clubs
- Mountains
- Outstanding schools
- High-end shopping
- Fine dining
- Boating
- Tennis
- Skiing
- Yachting
- Polo
- Racecar driving
- Hunting
- Ballroom dancing
- Exotic animals
- Antiques
- Horse racing
- Mountain climbing
- Hot air balloons
- Sky diving

- Scuba diving
- Art collecting
- High-stakes poker
- Winemaking
- Vintage cars
- Flying airplanes

If your listing is located near any of these attractions, be sure to include that information in the listing description. You should also include some high-resolution photos that show others enjoying that attraction. Just be sure to always market the luxury lifestyle when marketing a luxury listing.

12. Use High-End Marketing Materials

Rich people's extremely high standards lead them to expect everything they touch, hear and see to be spectacular. That means you can't send them cheap postcards with low-quality images and expect to capture new leads.

If you want to succeed as a luxury property agent, everything you use for marketing must be pristine and remarkable, including but not limited to:

- Your website
- Audio clips
- Videos
- Audiobooks
- Written content
- Graphics
- Social media
- Press releases
- Brochures
- Emails
- Guides

As an agent, you are a service provider. But as a luxury agent, you are literally serving the wealthy. That means you must tap into their passion for the luxury lifestyle to capture their attention. So, trust me when I say that concentrating on marketing the local lifestyle of the listing is the best way to market the listing itself.

7 Exceptionally Unique Ways to Market Luxury Real Estate

Atlanta's luxury real estate market is a very competitive one for agents and brokers alike. That means you have to be innovative and creative to compete in my market. This is especially true since the rise of the coronavirus has created a work-from-home trend leading to a greater demand for more space.

According to an Inman report on luxury home trends, three new demographics are taking over the high-end home buying scene:

1. **Explorers** – Looking for homes in small towns and out-of-the-way neighborhoods
2. **Resorters** – Now seeking to buy homes in their favorite vacationing spots
3. **New Suburbanites** – Purchasing homes in suburban communities that provide more:
    a. Property amenities
    b. Good schools
    c. Space

What does this mean for agents in the high-end homes industry? It gives you even more opportunities to make yourself stand out from other agents in your market. That means you need to not only market yourself, but you need to use exceptionally unique ways to market your listings as well.

Here are seven unique, actionable tips for marketing your luxury listings while making you shine above your local competitors:

1. Single Property Webpage or Website

This is where your website comes into play. Keep in mind that the ultra-wealthy like feeling special, especially since the amount they pay for home sell commissions can be enormous. So, make them feel well-cared for by dedicating an entire webpage to their property on your site.

Or, if you want to get really creative, purchase a unique domain name for the property and launch an entire site exclusively dedicated to it. Now, that's some high-end marketing!

Sounds complicated? Not really. Just have your web designer create a template for your luxury home clients and use it over and over again. All you have to do is change the text and visuals to match the listing itself.

Either way, use the webpage or website to showcase the home and its greatest, luxurious features. Be sure to use the highest quality videos and images that showcase the sophistication of the property. You can even take it up a notch and use drones to capture captivating aerial views, 3-D scans or 6-D renderings.

Here are the things you need to focus on when creating websites and webpages for high-end properties:

- Spectacular images
- Compelling videos
- Persuasive text content

All of these elements help potential buyers visually imagine themselves living in the upscale home. This compels them to virtually engage with the property, and eventually, you, as the listing agent.

2. Outsource to a Professional Copywriter

Speaking of persuasive text content… As a licensed real estate agent, you probably don't have the skills needed to write compelling text that speaks directly to your target buyers. Or maybe you do have writing skills but simply don't have the time to create captivating content that lures in qualified buyers.

So, why not hire a professional who specializes in writing content about luxury real estate?

Decision-Making focuses on two things:

1. Purchases are made using emotions
2. Purchases are justified using logic

Copywriters understand this and use the psychology behind it to write copy that induces emotions while providing readers with reassuring reasons for clicking on Calls-to-Action (CTA). They write text in conversational tones that entice site visitors to continue reading and want to click on CTAs like "Learn More" and "View More Images."

Agents tend to write property listings that are boring and straight factual. However, a professional copywriter can take that same copy and transform your listing descriptions into enticing, unique content, while infusing the perfect mix of SEO keywords to help the content rank higher in online searches.

3. Buy Newspaper Features

With all this talk about online marketing, I bet you never saw this one coming! Yes, newspaper features still work in the 2020s.

Digital marketing is the key to reaching the masses when marketing a luxury listing. However, you can still get a lot of coverage in international, national and local newspapers as long as they are major publications.

Keep in mind that there are still consumers out there who enjoy their morning cup of coffee with a newspaper. High-end real estate investors and buyers comb property listings in these publications.

Capture their attention quickly with double-page spreads featuring mesmerizing, eye-popping images of your luxury home listing.

4. Sponsor an Event VS an Open House

Open houses tend to draw in looky-loos who have no intention of buying or simply don't qualify for upscale homes. They are just curious to view such homes and basically, waste your time.

So, why not skip the ordinary open houses and host a private event to view the home instead? Here are some unique home-showing event ideas for you to think about:

- **Charity** – Find a cause your seller supports and host a charity event so others can also support the cause while viewing the property
- **Art Show** – Host an art show for local artists and have the artists donate portions of their proceeds to a local cause or charge guest cover charges and/or have them donate as well
- **Upscale Dance -** High-Net-Worth (HNW) consumers love dressing up for events like these, especially when they support local causes and showcase the upscale home's wide-open entertainment spaces
- **High-End Gala** – For an eco-friendly home, you can host a social event that allows attendees to sponsor the eco-friendly maintenance of a local location, such as a park or school

5. Produce a Digital Storybook

Your wealthy clients will be so impressed to see that you've created a digital storybook featuring their luxurious listing as the story's main character. This is one tool that's been proven to help increase online engagement. When professional produced with high-quality audio, your online storybook should:

- Be captivating
- Provoke emotion
- Deeply immersive

This is the perfect way to showcase a luxury home to potential buyers who are not in the local area. Allow your international and national buyers to enjoy a virtual walkthrough of the property to entice them to give you a call.

6. Step Up Your Direct Mail Game

Just imagine you're a homeowner in the middle of a divorce or some other life-changing moment. You're thinking about selling but just haven't taken the first step yet.

Then, suddenly, you're going through your mail and you see a postcard telling you that an agent has just sold a home in your local area… just blocks from you. As a homeowner, you may take this as a sign that *this* is the agent you need to call.

When done right, direct mail campaigns can definitely help you capture new leads. But don't waste your time or money sending out mundane postcards and letters that read like resumes. Most homeowners don't care about your certifications or licenses. And they definitely could care less about your active listings.

Instead, keep your mail from going directly into the trash by creating bonds with your recipients. Here are the goals you should aim for:

- **Frequently** – This allows you to become familiar to them, especially if you include a high-resolution image of yourself

- **Impactful** – Your mailers should bring value to the lives of your high-end homeowners, not simply sell them on selling
- **Trust** – Use your mail campaigns to build relationships with your recipients, so when they *are* ready to sell, you'll be their go-to-source

Quality Is Key with High-End Direct Mailers

Luxury homeowners deserve luxury direct mail. That means you need to purchase high-quality products that look and feel luxurious. Instead of a matte finish, invest the extra dollars for a high-end glossy finish for a more upscale look and feel.

You can even add a QR code to your mail material, especially postcards. Link it to your website for a creative way for your recipients to:

- Download your business card
- Respond to an exclusive invitation
- Order a Comparative Market Analysis (CMA)
- Schedule a call or online chat
- Download your digital seller's guide

Just keep in mind that whatever you send out needs to be valuable to the recipients. Rich people have no need for free ink pens or calendars with your picture and logos all over them. So, stick to high-quality direct mail campaigns that educate and/or entertain rather than sell your brand.

7. Price Just Below Market Value

Many newbies shy away from this idea simply because they want to sell homes for the highest prices possible to collect the highest commissions possible. However, this is a great strategy for getting the listing sold fast.

If your local market is currently flooded with upscale listings, pricing the listing *just* below market value could be the boost you need. This opens the listing up to even more qualified buyers while creating a competitive listing that could lead to a bidding war. When this happens, the price automatically increases as the war continues.

This luxury property marketing strategy is not meant for all listings. But in certain situations, it could mean the difference between selling fast and dealing with an expired listing later.

6 Tips for New Agents Marketing Luxury Homes

When it comes to affluent consumers, about half of them are **brand neutral**. Yes, you read that right! That means that you have a 50/50 chance of these high-end clients keeping you as their trusted real estate agent.

So, as a newbie, you must ask yourself these questions:

- How do you make sure that your well-to-do clients keep using your services?
- How can you attract new affluent clients and get them to remain your clients?
- How do you get your current clients to refer you to other wealthy consumers ready to sell or buy?

Here are six tips to help you come up with the answers, which I'll break down further in a moment:

1. Locate the perfect client
2. Narrow down your target market
3. Understand the problem you solve
4. Learn the uniqueness of your clients
5. Serve your upscale clients the way *they* prefer being served
6. Be Hyper-Sensitive about Image

Now, let's dig deeper into the five principles.

1. Locate the Perfect Client

In many industries, it's sufficient to create a basic profile of what your ideal client looks like. However, in the luxury home arena, this won't do. Rich clients expect VIP service, which requires you to treat each individual potential client as a unique person. As a matter of fact, they *expect* it.

A basic profile gives you an idea of who you prefer working with and who you don't. When "courting" a potential client in the luxury market, dig deeper and find out what motivates that client to move forward.

2. Narrow Down Your Target Market

Of course, your main target market is luxury homeowners and buyers. However, narrowing down your focus allows you to become an industry expert in a specialized niche. Here are some ideas to help you understand this concept better:

- First-time high-end home buyers
- Seasoned luxury home buyers or sellers
- Environmentally conscious affluent buyers or sellers
- Buyers seeking homes over $3 million
- Sellers selling homes over $5 million
- Young, wealthy buyers or sellers who prefer discreetly rich communities
- International high-end vacation home buyers
- Sellers of brand-new apartments or upscale penthouses or condos
- Celebrity buyers or sellers, such as movie stars or sports figures
- Successful millennial buyers or sellers

3. Understand the Problem You Solve

Not every client is alike. That means each one has her/his own specific needs and pain points. Your potential clients are searching for an agent simply because they have problems that need to be solved. To win them over, you must show that you have the solutions to those problems.

It takes much more than marketing yourself as an agent who links qualified buyers with high-end home sellers. Why? Well, let's face it. That's what every agent does.

You need to take it a step further to determine the specific problems you solve as a luxury real estate agent. Think about your past transactions and ask yourself:

- What did you do exceptionally well?
- Specifically, what made a lasting impression on past clients?
- What have your referring clients been saying about you?

Don't have the answers to all of these questions? No problem. There are ways to get the answers from your past upscale clients, such as:

- Give each one a call and start a conversation about their experience with you
- Create an email campaign that includes a brief survey about their experience
- Send out postcards with a QR code that links to an online survey they can complete

Now, you can use this information to create a spreadsheet or database to capture this data. Use it to create your magic formula for problem-solving for luxury home clients. Then, ask yourself these additional questions and incorporate the answers into your problem-solving statement:

- What category do you fall into?
- What makes you different from your competitors?
- Who are your target clients?

- Where can they be found?
- When do they need your help?
- Why are you the best go-to source for them?

Once crafted, your statement is complete. Here's an example:

- **Who** – Millennials seeking homes over $3 million
- **What** – An innovate realtor who educates sellers during the transaction
- **When** – Before having children
- **Where** – In upscale Atlanta communities
- **How** – By finding prestigious homes in areas filled with amenities
- **Why** – They work hard and want to play even harder

4. Learn the Uniqueness of your Clients

You have narrowed down your target market and determined the specific problem you solve. Now, it's time to determine what makes your clients so unique if you want to make an impression that lasts forever.

There are a number of benefits when taking interest in knowing the uniqueness of potential and current clients. This could lead you to schedule a viewing of a specific listing over another simply because the buyer has children. Both listings have swimming pools, but only one is enclosed.

Using the FORD Method

As a luxury real estate agent, you need to create a solid foundation of trust with potential clients at networking events and upscale parties. The FORD method is an effective way to have good conversations with prospective clients. FORD stands for:

- Family

- Occupation
- Recreation
- Dreams

The key is to use this technique to ask questions that help you get to know these consumers. Then, you *must* be interested in their responses while following up with more questions. Be sure to listen closely to their responses. This will help you discover unique opportunities to help solve problems they are currently having.

Here's an example of a FORD Method conversation:

- **Are you married?** *Yes, I've been married for 22 years.*
- **Do you have any kids?** *Yes, we have four children.*
- **What are their names and ages?** *Jasmine is 21. Hannah is 19. Chris is 15. And Briana is 11.*
- **Are Jasmine and Hannah in college?** *Well, Jasmine dropped out to have a baby. But Hannah started her sophomore year at Alabama State this semester.*
- **Where do they live?** *Jasmine and her baby live with us. Hannah has an apartment near campus.*
- **With you living in Georgia, do you get to see Hannah often?** *Not really. Although she does come to stay with us for spring, winter and summer breaks. But we really don't have the room for her with the baby and all. So, she takes over our living room when she visits.*

And there you have it! A problem you can help solve!

In my case, I own a piece of high-end property with a couple of partners that we lease out as a short-term rental in the local area. So, I would make a follow-up call right before summer starts to offer the rental to her. This allows the daughter to continue living in her own space while freeing the homeowners' living room up for the summer.

However, in your case, you could do the following:

- Locate a high-end, short-term rental in the area that meets the daughter's needs
- Find a luxury condo for sale near a college campus that can be rented out to students during the school year and used to house the daughter during the summer months

5. Serve Them How *They* Prefer Being Served

As a whole, upscale buyers have extremely high standards and expectations for their agents, such as:

- Experienced and established
- Well-known and respected locally
- Very educated about the area where they want to buy
- Has an extensive network of high-end service providers
- Shows she/he understands their current needs
- Has a luxury home specialist certification or accreditation

And these conditions are just the beginning. If you truly want to separate your brand from other upscale real estate agents in your area, you *must* concentrate on how you make your prospective clients *feel.* Here are some tips:

Listen Attentively

To become successful in the high-end industry, you must forge healthy relationships with your wealthy clientele. They must come to like, know and trust you if you want to seal the deal.

So, how do you get these prosperous consumers to like you? That's simple. Just make them feel special by giving them your full, undivided attention. Then, respond to the things they say empathetically. This also helps you learn even more about them, which helps you provide a more personal touch.

Make It Personal

Think about this scenario:

- The home sells for $3.5 million
- At 6%, the agent's commission is $210,000

That's a pretty big commission to give to an agent who doesn't make them feel special. They also want to feel like their listing is special to you as well. So, be sure to create listing descriptions that showcase the amazing features of the mansion that not only entice buyers but also impresses the sellers.

For example:

This mansion features an elegant pollinator garden and multiple raised garden beds for gardening lovers. For cooking enthusiasts, you'll love the sub-zero smart refrigerator and matching smart oven, both with built-in Wi-Fi.

Don't Be Predictable

Rich people are used to getting exceptional service that goes above and beyond their expectations. You must provide this same higher level of service to make a lasting impression. Instead of being predictable, match their expectations by doing unexpected things that make you look thoughtful to improve your relationships with these high-end clients.

For example, let's say you're driving a couple around a specific community they're interested in. Make a great impression by treating them to lunch at one of the local hotspots in the area. They'll be thrilled to learn that you've already made a reservation for a private table. This also gives you another chance to chat with them about their needs and local amenities that meet those needs.

Here are some other out-of-the-box ideas for wooing your clients:

- Schedule a tour of the local country club and introduce them to the manager
- Have a special "welcome home" gift delivered to them on moving day, such as a bottle of Dom Perignon
- Offer to host an upscale housewarming party for the new homeowners and have it catered with cheese, wine and all the fixings

6. Be Hyper-Sensitive about Image

Image is *everything* in the luxury real estate industry. The impression a home makes on potential buyers is key to selling a listing.

The Listing's Image

A luxury home buyer is not your typical buyer. Instead, they tend to become extremely fixated on minor imperfections in a home that other consumers may consider stunning. Therefore, the home and its landscape must be in pristine, immaculate conditions.

So, to improve the impression buyers get from the listing, have the property professionally staged. And be sure to a hire professional real estate photographer and videographer to take stunning visuals of the property.

Your Image Matters Too

The impression *you* make also matters. You must look like money and spend money to make money in this business. Wear professional clothing and polished shoes that give you the look of luxury to match your upscale clientele.

Your vehicle should also look the part, so your clients connect with it. High-end agents shouldn't ride around in economy cars if they want to impress their wealthy clients. Instead, you need a clean, comfortable SUV or sedan that's easy for clients to enter and exit.

Also, time is money. And prosperous people don't like wasting either one. So, always be on time or even earlier than expected when meeting with them.

Your Marketing Image

What type of image does your marketing portray? To succeed in the luxury real estate market, you must build long-lasting relationships long before any transaction occurs. In other words, as I've stated before, the prospective client needs to like, know and trust you for the relationship to work.

This all starts with your marketing tactics. You need to make impressions that are long-lasting and positive if you plan to attract new clients, retain existing ones and earn valuable referrals.

Luxury home marketing follows the same basic concepts used by other agents to market lower-end homes. The big difference is that you'll need to follow *much* higher standards to get affluent sellers and buyers to like, know and trust you. Once again, your marketing strategy needs to be personal, personalized and all about the client.

So, how do you personalize a client's experience with you? Here are some tips:

- Take a personal interest in the client. Ask relevant questions and listen attentively to the answers. Learn all you can about the client because your discoveries can help you find the perfect home to meet the client's needs and desires.
- Always care about the client's own personal comfort to ensure the consumer feels special. Find creative ways to exceed her/his expectations.

- Invest in marketing material that's personalized specifically for your brand. This could be anything from eBooks and books to magazines and email newsletters. Personally, I use a company called Authorify for this.

No matter which tactics you use, make sure that your marketing materials are as high-end as the luxury listing you're trying to sell. Marketing upscale homes is all about impressing wealthy buyers and sellers by making a positive and memorable first impression that lasts forever.

Good Luck to All New Luxury Real Estate Agents

Selling luxury real estate in the 2020s takes much more innovation than it did twenty years ago. To be successful in this industry, you must not only face your fears head-on but you must be prepared to embrace changes of many kinds:

- Ethics changes
- Law changes
- Market changes
- Statistic changes
- Trend changes
- Development changes
- Advertising changes
- Marketing changes

Aim to be that great agent who continuously strives to find innovative and creative ways to market your brand and business. This helps ensure you capture more new leads and hold on to clients you've worked with during the past. So, be sure to keep learning about new industry-related technologies. And keep looking for ways to incorporate them into your daily business practices.

Always keep up with what's happening in your local luxury market. Read any and everything you can find related to the industry. And never, ever let your fear of learning and trying new things slow down your process of becoming a successful agent to high-end clients.